Honey In My Shoes

Flora Currie McCallum

Given to Chris Whitaker by Flora McRae McLaurin — March 2005

Text
Copyright © 2002 Flora Currie McCallum

All rights reserved. No part of this book may be reproduced or transmitted in any form or by any means, electronic or mechanical, including photocopying, recording, or by any information storage system, without permission in writing from the publisher.

Published by Warren Publishing, Inc.

ISBN 1-886057-91-5

Library of Congress Catalog Number 97-062246

Printed in the United States of America

Warren Publishing, Inc.
19809 North Cove Road
Cornelius, North Carolina 28031

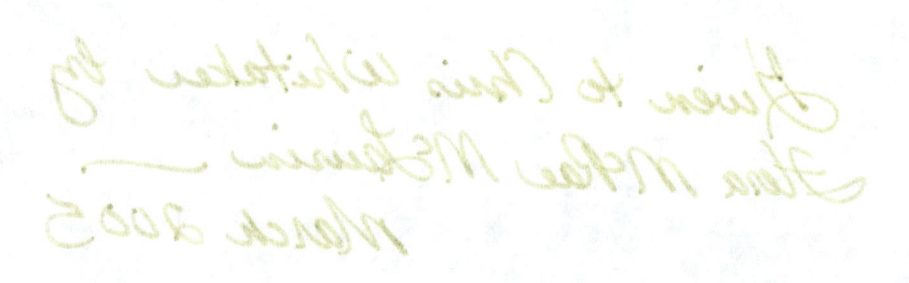

Dedication

To Lewood, Will, and Victor, because they listened patiently as I read each poem to them.

To the memory of my mother, Elizabeth Brown Harriss Currie, a poet, librarian and teacher.

These poems are the result of memories, thoughts, observation and imagination.

Flora

About The Poet

I was brought up in the small Scottish town of Maxton, N.C. I attended the local schools and afterward went to Greensboro, N.C., where I graduated from Woman's College of the University of North Carolina, majoring in Clothing and Textiles and Home Economics Education. I worked as an assistant to a dress designer in Charlotte, N.C. and taught Home Economics courses in high schools from the foothills of the mountains to the coastal plains of North Carolina, and at St. Andrews Presbyterian College in Laurinburg, N.C.

My interest in poetry was influenced early on by the mere presence of my mother, by my fourth grade teacher, by English courses at Woman's College, and by the works of John Charles McNeill.

I married Lewood McCallum, Jr., a farmer from Rowland, N.C. This is where we raised our two sons. Living on a farm in the beautiful countryside of Rowland provided inspiration and thoughts for my poetry.

I must give credit to my father, William Martin Currie, who was full of wit and humor and had a profound appreciation of nature. All through my life, it never surprised me when he would teasingly ask me which I would rather do, carry a frog around in my pocket or walk around all day with *Honey In My Shoes*.

                                        Flora Currie McCallum
                                        Rowland, N.C.
                                        August 2002

Honey In My Shoes

Tiny Dancing Slippers

1. Honey In My Shoes
2. Night Hour
3. Daddy Wa-Wa-Wa
4. Sunny Daffodils
5. Aunt Lila
6. Stomp
7. Timmy and Lisa
8. Suppertime
9. Maude
11. An August Morning on One Man's Plantation

Sensible Shoes

15. A House on a Hill
17. Ida's Rooster
18. Hint of Autumn
19. The Frolic Of The Leaves
20. Gingko Tree
21. Winter Leaves
22. December Song
23. The Snow Banquet
25. The Brown Thrasher
26. Spring's Promise
27. A Miracle At Mitchell Swamp

28. Dogwood's High Fashion
29. Summer Dress
30. The Farmer
31. Old McCormick House

Diamonds on my Soles

35. Dance at the Medallion
37. Isaac and Grace
38. The Holly Grove
39. Old House
40. High on the Hill
41. Where I Live
42. Andrew and Olivia
43. Aunt Molly, Aunt Dolly, Aunt Maggie and Aunt Kate
44. Honey In My Shoes

Tiny Dancing Slippers

Honey In My Shoes

Life has much to offer.
Every single day I must choose
Whether to carry a frog around in my pocket
All day,
or to wear
Honey In My Shoes.

Night Hour

In the cold blackness of the winter sky
    The moon slipped into its pocket,
While I lay sleepless on my cot
    Fingering my golden locket.

Like brilliants studded in onyx, the stars
Blinked the night hour slowly away,
While I lay sleepless on my cot
Until the first gray light of day.

Daddy Wa-Wa-Wa

Daddy Wa-Wa-Wa
Daddy Wa Wee,
Across the wood, the chant was heard
Daddy Wa-Wa-Wa, Daddy Wa Wee.
Distinct and clear was every word,
But, all so strange and new to me.
A sing-song sound, a sing-song sound,
But, all so strange and new to me.
A revelation,
A telling tale, the chant cried,
For these were children playing
Age-old hide.
Daddy Wa-Wa-Wa, Daddy Wa Wee
Daddy Wa-Wa-Wa, Daddy Wa Wee.

Sunny Daffodils

In early spring every year
I could count on it,
Yet, it was always a surprise;
He would come into my kitchen
And hand me a tightly clasped
Fistful of sunny daffodils.

Aunt Lila

I remember the dusty brown
    of Aunt Lila's bare feet,
How in the summertime
She could let her soles go free.
But in the winter, not by choice,
She must cover her whole self
With cast-off garments someone
    else did not want.
She was an old Negress of
    a long ago school,
Never again to be seen in actuality,
But only in reminiscings expressed
    on paper in someone else's words
    or of scenes brushed on a canvas.

Stomp

In childish treble the word was spoken,
Today in memory only a token.
In yesteryear the plea was made,
Granted only when rules were obeyed,
For a beverage delightful to behold
Was coffee and sugar-laced milk
Served warm, not cold.
Then biscuit was pressed into the milk,
Making nourishment as smooth as silk.
Upon entering the house from meadow romp
The children enjoyed what they called
Stomp.

Timmy and Lisa

Timmy and Lisa were tree frogs two,
Together they lived in an iron pipe
      the winter through.
They ate and slept and
      I'm sure did woo,
Just as tree frogs two
      are expected to do.
Ugh Hm! Yes!
Just as I told you…
      I said they'd woo.
Now there are tree frogs three
      Instead of just two!

Suppertime

In the dying heat, the sausage
Shriveled in the grease,
While volcanoes bubbled on the
Surface of the yellow grits.
Buttermilk biscuits rose tall and
Brown in the oven
As the blue spatterware coffee pot
Danced in a frenzy on the stove.
Altogether the aromas wafted through
The air and announced

Suppertime!

Maude

Her name was Maude
She strolled through the camellias
    in the late afternoon.
Her hair was burnt gold in
    the sun's slanting beams,
Her cheeks were red and her
    lips were too.
Her long flowing voile print gown
    rippled around her ankles
    as she moved.
She sipped a sparkling martini
    from which the olive had already
    been removed.
Her other hand held a
Long keen amber holder which
    encased an unfiltered-tipped
            cigarette.

At age ten, to me this was the
Ultimate, the epitome, the essence
Of glamour and sophistication
And which I aspired to be, at
Least in part, if ever in this
World I could be grown.

An August Morning On One Man's Plantation

Toadstools dot the dewy grass,
No sun is up in the sky.
August days soon will pass.
On time we can rely.

A pungent aroma filters the air,
It's the hope of one man's tomorrow,
The yellow leaf: foe or fare,
No trouble would he borrow.

Sensible Shoes

A House on a Hill

I always wanted a house on a hill,
A big white frame house,
Where families had lived before
And where memories linger still
In every room and corner.

I always wanted a house on a hill
With tall, tall chimneys,
With a fireplace in every room,
With mantels where stockings can hang,
Where laughter of children
       echoes from the past.

I always wanted a house on a hill
With lots of big windows,
Where sunlight is invited in,
Where the wind whistles
       around its corners at night
And I won't be afraid,
Because it is what I wanted.
I always wanted a house on a hill

With lots of great big rooms,
Where there is "wasted" space,
Where I can place an old trunk
Or a washstand with a bowl and pitcher.

I always wanted a house on a hill,
A big white frame house.
I want to name my house one day
With a name worthy of it.
One day I'll do just that.
When I can call it *Our House.*

                        written for Stuart
                        and Leah J. McCallum

Ida's Rooster

Ida's rooster struts the yard
That oozes between his gnarled toes;
From Chaucerian line as some old bard
He announces the new day in perfect prose.

Hint of Autumn

Scarlet leaves at Autumn's birth
Seem strangely premature,
For summer sun is setting still,
Its heat we yet endure.

The Frolic Of The Leaves

In verdant glory the leaves provide umbrella
For all the creatures who would enjoy,
But in brief season now each woodsy fellow
Must seek his haven by cunning employ.
For now the leaves in multi-hue
Detach themselves from twig and limb
And gracefully fall in the autumn dew
And leave the tree all bare and grim.
Reds and yellows frolic and frenzy in chase,
Or twirl in a whirlwind high in the air.
Finally they float earthward
And settle in place
And die in their beauty there.

Gingko Tree

Gingko tree, O, Ginkgo tree,
You're a lady with a million fans,
Waving to and fro in fashion free,
Bowing and swaying to the wind's demands.
Vibrant and royal in your precious summer jade,
You coyly spread your full limbs
And nestle songbirds in your luscious shade.
Briefly, as if it were one of Nature's whims
You don your golden autumnal gown
And for a season
You are the sunshine in our land.
But soon at your roots there on the ground,
Suddenly and shamelessly you drop
      every
           last
               fan!

Winter Leaves

The brown winter leaves ran up the hill
And when they reached the top
They turned around and ran back down
As though they could not stop.

I watched them as they ran
Like people in a crowd
Each one keeping his position
Led by nose or intuition.

December Song

December brings a Christmas song
Of a chill and starlit night,
Of an angel and wise men
And a glorious guiding light.
December brings a Christmas song
Of a Holy Babe born that night,
Of the Prince of Peace who came in starlight.
Angels announced His birth
      with trumpet and with horn
To let the Earth know our Savior had been born.
December brings a Christmas song
That never shall grow old.
It is a melody that warms our hearts
With love each time that it is told,
When December brings Peace on Earth in song.

The Snow Banquet

Our table was spread in snow of pure white.
All the birds were the invited guests.
From the swamp they came in wavy flight,
From the fields they flew eagerly to the fest.
All those who came were beautifully dressed
In harmonious garments so expertly pressed.

The tiny chickadee wore his black velvet cap,
So jauntily set and it had no strap.
The sparrow, all frenzied,
    wore his everyday brown,
While the cardinal in scarlet wore the crown.
Sometimes over powering, the gawky blue jay
Wore his coat and vest of soft gray.
In his banker's gray suit
    the junco was so polite he dare not encumber
    his friends who came to the table
To partake of the morsels and join in the babel.

Strangely enough the small gay purple finch
Will sit by the blue jay without a flinch.
The friendly little finch wears his rosy red
Both on his breast and atop his tiny head.
All sat at the banquet table except the towee,
Who dined under the table
    with the greatest of glee.

The atmosphere was pleasant as they
Consumed the ration,
Until the mocking birds swooped in to
Claim their station.

The Brown Thrasher

The Brown thrasher wears a speckled vest
And strolls in a cutaway coat.
He's always dressed his very best
When the farmer's seed corn
Slides down his throat.

Spring's Promise

Stark against the steel gray sky
Bare limbs quiver in January's blast.
In the bitter cold songbirds cry,
But spring's promise at long last
Is already budding where songbirds fly.

A Miracle At Mitchell Swamp

An eerie feeling came upon me
As my attention was drawn
To the one bright spot
In the swamp.
The sun had crept around
To the opening
Made by a power company.
It was like a spotlight
Directed exactly upon
The sanguine-tipped spear
That arose mysteriously
From the dark, murky and
Duck-weed crowded water
Of the creek.
The spear, like a knight's sword
Just drawn from a felled enemy
Was the crimson colored lobelia,
A rare wildflower,
A miracle at Mitchell Swamp.

Dogwood's High Fashion

The dogwood wears her summer green
In the sultriest days of all.
She flashes her gayest colors
Of reds and purples in the fall.
But winter brings a somber mood
When she wears a colorless face.
But, ah, in spring she's best of all
When she adorns her gown of whitest lace.

Summer's Dress

Summer's dress is silken green,
Splashed with gold and yellow.
Royal purple stands graceful and tall
Forming her hemline border.
Daisies at the bodice closure
Button to her sunny face,
While lavender wisteria
Wraps a sash around her tiny waist.

The Farmer

I heard it said, back in the thirties,
When the farmer came to town,
He wore one gallus up and the
    other hanging down.
Now, why do you suppose he dressed
    in such array?
Was it by choice or the style of the day?
I think it was an earmark of his spirit,
    for times were bad.
His heart was heavy and he was feeling sad.
Now, I expect today if you go downtown,
Once again you'll find the farmer
With one gallus up and the
    other hanging down.

Old McCormick House

Each year after the harvest
The old weathered house is in plain view.
In Civil War days it housed a large
    and well known family.
Years and the elements have taken their toll
    on the long ago vacated home.
It is in a dilapidated state.
All that remains are the rooms, which were
    the kitchen, the keeping room, a long
    bedroom on one side and a tin-covered
    porch whose posts have fallen,
    leaving the roof at a curious angle.
A massive fireplace, surrounded by
    crumbling brick, still is in evidence.
One can imagine Christmas stockings hung
    above on a mantel that has disappeared.
The only shutters that are left hang
    by one H-hinge.

Outside, an aged black walnut tree's
　　branches reach through the glassless
　　front window as if searching
　　for its family that has long departed
　　this good earth.

Diamonds on my Soles

Dance at the Medallion

The other night when I couldn't rest in bed
I came downstairs to sleep in the chair instead,
Thought I'd be bored, awake and alone all night
But much to my surprise it was a complete
      delight.
Through the window moonlight cast a soft glow
      in preparation for the evening's show.
I was enjoying the beauty of the rug, quietness,
      and light,
When I heard a tiny noise on each
      side of the room.
I looked to the left, I looked to the right,
All of a sudden there was an unbelievable sight.
Two small mice ran to the
      medallion, the center of the rug,
He bowed, she curtsied and they gave
      each other a hug.

Two steps back from each other they took
And twirled away into the darkness under
        a chair.
Again they scampered to the middle of the rug,
He bowed, she curtsied,
        and they gave each other a hug.
They leapt into the air and pirouetted about;
They danced all night until they both gave out.

Isaac and Grace

Isaac and Grace run hand in hand
Across the grass to Fairy Land
Where the swings soar to the heavenly sky,
Where the slide is wide and high.
Flaxen curls bounce in the sun
Here and there wherever they run.
Miss Scarlet rests in the shade nearby
Protecting the children with her watchful eye.
Through sky-blue eyes they see the world,
This little boy, this tiny girl.
    Isaac and Grace.

    Written for David and Sarah Hendrix

The Holly Grove

Come with me to the holly grove
Down to the deep of the wood,
Where free souls would wander and rove
And where nature is green and good.

No sidewalks wind to the busy street,
No wheels drown the sound of the bird,
Only the peace of the forest replete,
Only the pines whisper a word.

Old House

Old house stands vacant and lonely now
Where life once pressed its seams.
Same old oak tree bends its bough
Across the ancient beams.

Old House stands gray and proud
As though life were still inside.
Laughter of children echoes loud
Where memories of love abide.

High on the Hill

High on the hill will be my grave,
Where the moon glows cool,
And the sun rises high,
And the birds fly free,
High on the hill they will bury me.

High on the hill will be my grave,
Where the earth and the sky meet,
Where the wildflowers grow and will cover me,
Where the winds blow fresh,
And the birds fly free,
High on the hill they will bury me.

Where I Live

I live where the wild fern grows,
The elephant ear and turtlehead,
Where the cypress knee stands
Like sentinels in the swamp.
My home is where the blue flag flourishes,
The venus looking glass and blue-eyed grass,
And where the knotweed and vervain
Grace our beaten paths.
I live where life is peaceful and serene,
Where the hawk circles and soars
And where the dove is
At peace in her nest.

Andrew and Olivia

Do we have grandchildren?
Why, of course we do!
There are two year old Olivia
And four year old Andrew.
Andrew is the spark that lights our day.
Olivia is the dewdrop that melts
    our hearts away.
Andrew is laughter in perpetual motion.
While Olivia's penetrating gaze is like a
    placid ocean.
Together they are a delight to behold,
What more can we ask when we get old?

Aunt Molly, Aunt Dolly, Aunt Maggie and Aunt Kate

Aunt Molly, Aunt Dolly, Aunt Maggie and
 Aunt Kate,
Each had a hand in my ultimate fate.
Although around my friends I may not show it,
All of my kinfolks full well know it,
For their lives too had the ultimate fate
Of being influenced by
Aunt Molly, Aunt Dolly, Aunt Maggie and
 Aunt Kate.

Honey In My Shoes

Life has much to offer.
Every single day I must choose
Whether to carry a frog around in my pocket
All day,
or to wear
Honey In My Shoes.